WE'RE TALKING ABOUT
ALCOHOL

JENNY BRYAN

Wayland

Series editor: Catherine Baxter
Book editor: Louise Woods
Design: John Christopher

First published in 1995 by Wayland Publishers Ltd
61 Western Road, Hove, East Sussex, BN3 1JD, England

© Copyright 1995 Wayland (Publishers) Ltd.

British Library Cataloguing in Publication Data

Bryan, Jenny
We're Talking About Alcohol
I. TITLE
362.292
ISBN 0-7502-1643-3

Typeset by Strong Silent Type
Printed and bound by Canale & C.S.p.A, Turin

Picture Acknowledgements
Cephas: 6 (Stuart Boreham); Greg Evans Photo Library: 14; David Hoffman: 12, 27: Impact: 22 (Piers Cavendish), 28 (Simon Shepheard); Tizzie Knowles: 4 (top and bottom), 5 (top and bottom), 8, 9, 10, 15, 19, 20, 21, 25; Life File: 24 (Emma Lee); Peter Newark: 16; Christine Osborne Pictures: 26; Peter Sanders: 17; Science Photo Library: 13 (John Greim); WPL: 4 (middle), 7.

Most of the people featured in this book are models.

Contents

Do you drink?	4
Where alcohol comes from	6
How alcohol affects the body	8
What happens if you drink too much	10
Too much, too often	12
The laws on drinking	14
Prohibition	16
The risks people take	18
Alcohol and violence	20
Drinking and driving	22
Mixing alcohol and drugs	24
Alcohol and the environment	26
Drinking sensibly	28
Glossary	30
Further information	31
Index	32

Do you drink?

Annie is nine; her mum lets her have a few sips out of her wine glass at lunch time every Sunday. She's been doing it for some time. Annie doesn't actually like it much but thinks it's very grown up. Anyway, lots of her friends at school say they drink much more.

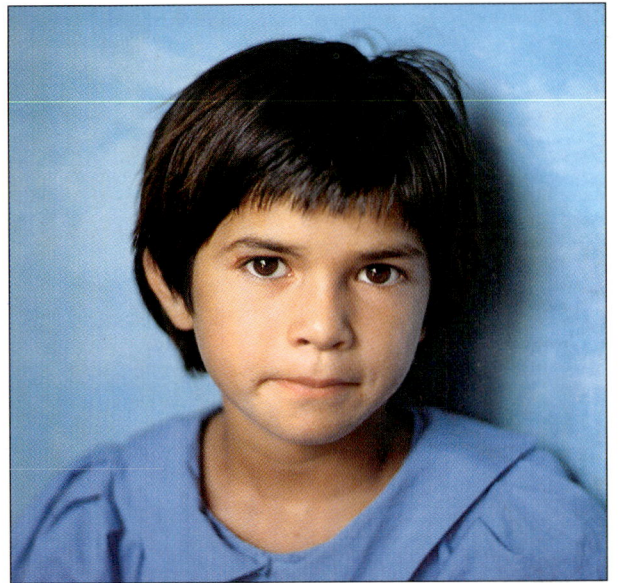

▲ Annie

Janet got so drunk when she went to a party that she didn't really know what she was doing. A boy took her home in his car and they had sex. Janet really wishes it hadn't happened and is worried she could be pregnant.

▲ Terry

Terry was very sick this morning. He and some twelve-year-old friends drank several cans of cider last night and Terry was very drunk. Luckily, his friends took him home but his dad was very angry and said he must stay in all weekend.

▼ Janet

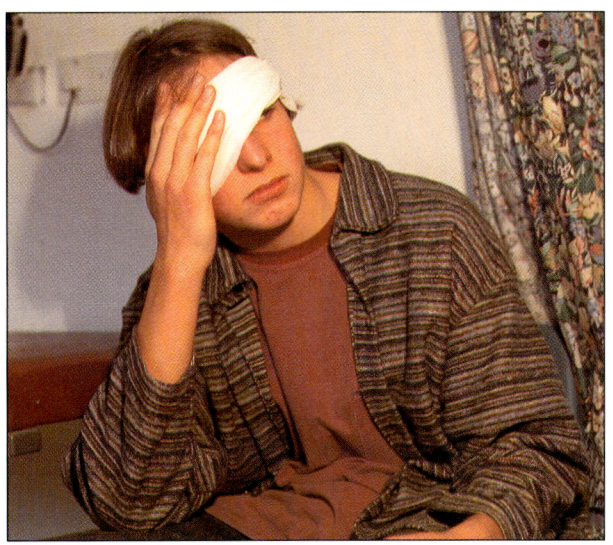

▲ John's brother

John's older brother is in hospital. He got into a fight outside a pub last week and someone hit him over the head with a bottle. He was unconscious for two days and the doctors are worried he may have lost the sight in one eye.

Sharon's mum was in a car accident on Saturday. It wasn't her fault — she swerved when a little girl ran in front of her car. She missed the child but knocked a cyclist off his bike. When the police came they found that Sharon's mum had too much alcohol in her blood and she was put in a cell in the police station.

Luckily, the cyclist wasn't hurt badly. But Sharon's mum will lose her driving licence and could get sent to prison.

Do you drink? Do you know anyone who has got into trouble with alcohol, like John's older brother or Sharon's mum? What about Janet — do you know anyone like her?

In this book you will discover a lot more about what happens when people drink. Alcohol is a strong drug and it affects your body and your mind. This book isn't against drinking, but it will give you the facts about alcohol so you can think about whether you want to drink or not.

▼ Sharon's mum

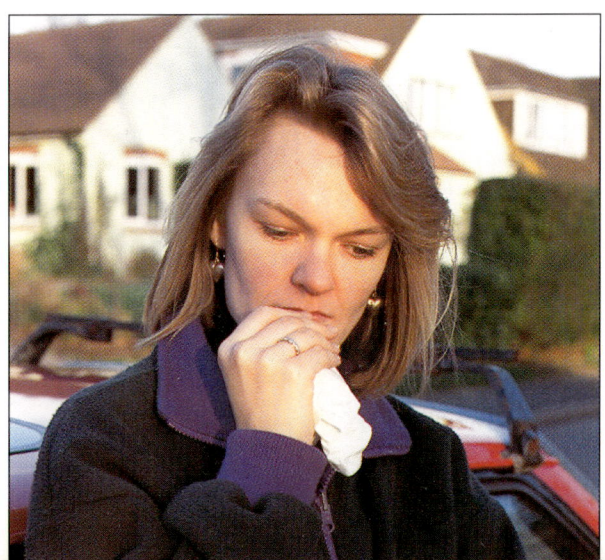

Where alcohol comes from

▲ Here the hops are sorted and weighed before being made into beer.

The chemical name of the alcohol we drink is ethyl alcohol, or ethanol. There are other alcohols, such as methyl alcohol, or methanol. But they are poisonous and are not used in drinks.

You can make alcoholic drinks from lots of different things. Wine, port and sherry come from grapes which are grown on vines.

Beer gets its flavour from hop plants and whisky is made from barley. Other drinks are also made from grains like barley, and then have fruit juices added to make them taste good.

Whatever plant is used, a process called fermentation is needed to produce the alcohol. Microbes called yeasts which live in the grapes or grains or are added to them, turn the sugars or starch into alcohol.

For example, to make wine, grapes are crushed so that yeast on the grape skins ferments the sugars in the juices.

Beer and whisky are made from barley, malt, yeast and water. In fact, beer is mostly water. Whisky is stronger, but still has a lot of water in it.

None of the things people normally drink are made entirely of alcohol. If they were, people would get drunk very quickly.

▲ Many vineyards have been in the same family for hundreds of years. Each generation looks after the vines and protects them from disease.

How alcohol affects the body

If you have a drink you will feel the effects very quickly. About ten or fifteen minutes after you swallow it, the alcohol will have gone from your stomach into your bloodstream. Once it's in your bloodstream, alcohol can go all around your body.

You'll probably get a warm feeling as the alcohol spreads. At first, it's rather nice – you may feel more confident. But if you keep drinking you'll start to feel hot and your face will go red. That's because blood is travelling through your veins faster than normal, trying to lose heat through your skin.

By then, the alcohol will have reached your brain. Your brain controls everything that goes on in your body – your eyes, your ears, your arms, your legs. So if you mess about with your brain it's not surprising that you lose control. The more you drink, the more this will happen.

▲ When you're out with friends it can be difficult to know exactly how much you've had to drink.

If you've been with adults who are drinking you'll probably have noticed that they talk louder and wave their arms around a lot. They often think they are being very funny so they laugh a lot. They think they are in control of themselves. But they can't concentrate very well. If you set them a test, they'd be rather slow.

If they keep drinking they will start to slur their words and their eyesight will become blurred. They'll find it difficult to walk straight across a room. They may bump into furniture and knock things over.

These things happen to different people at different times when they are drinking. Some people can drink quite a lot before they fall over, others much less. But each time they drink too much they kill some brain cells. They also kill cells in their liver.

No one knows how much people can drink before they damage their body. One or two drinks every few days may even be good for the heart. But drinking a lot makes you ill and getting drunk makes you look silly.

▶ Once a lot of alcohol is in your body, it's too late to stop it making you feel ill.

What happens if you drink too much

Terry felt very stupid the day after he got drunk. He also felt very ill. He had a hangover.

If you drink too much you may not fall over, but you may be very sick. At the back of your brain there is a centre which controls being sick. When you drink too much, messages go backwards and forwards between your stomach and this part of your brain.

When Terry drank too much cider his brain and stomach sent messages to each other and made him sick. The cider also made his brain cells thirsty – they didn't have enough water in them. This gave Terry a dreadful headache the day after he got drunk. All day, his head thumped and his stomach churned. He couldn't eat. Even the smell of food made him feel sick.

▼ Painkillers can help a headache, but they won't cure a hangover. It may be a long time before Terry feels better.

Terry's mum gave him some paracetamol for his headache and that made him feel a bit better. But his weekend was ruined because he wasn't allowed to go out with his friends, and he felt too ill anyway.

In fact, he had been feeling pretty miserable even before he got home and his dad had been cross. Terry thought alcohol would make him happy, not sad. Lots of people get this wrong, just like Terry. In fact, after the first few drinks, alcohol makes people depressed. If you're already feeling down, it doesn't cheer you up. It makes you feel worse.

Terry's other mistake was drinking without eating. Alcohol gets into the bloodstream much more quickly if you don't eat. Having a meal won't stop you getting drunk, but the alcohol affects you more slowly. You also tend to drink more slowly if you are eating and notice the effects the alcohol is having on your body and your feelings.

Too much, too often

Most adults have had too much to drink at some time in their lives – and wished they hadn't. But people who often drink too much can do themselves a lot of harm. They may also upset their families and friends. If they don't stop drinking too much they may lose their job, their home and everything that is important to them.

In large amounts, alcohol damages the liver. The liver is the

▼ This man has to sleep on the streets. He has lost his home because of problems with alcohol.

organ which processes the body's waste products. If it doesn't work properly, poisons build up in the body and make you very ill. They can even kill.

Alcohol can also damage the brain and nervous system. People who drink a lot find it hard to concentrate and remember things. They can't work properly. They don't eat properly and they feel ill a lot of the time.

People who cannot do without a lot of alcohol are called alcoholics. They may need alcohol so much that they have to drink all day. If they don't get a drink when they need one, they suffer withdrawal symptoms. This means they may shake, hear voices or think that people are plotting against them. They can make their families and friends very unhappy.

Alcoholics need help to sort out their problems. Some hospitals have clinics to help people find out why they drink too much and how to drink less.

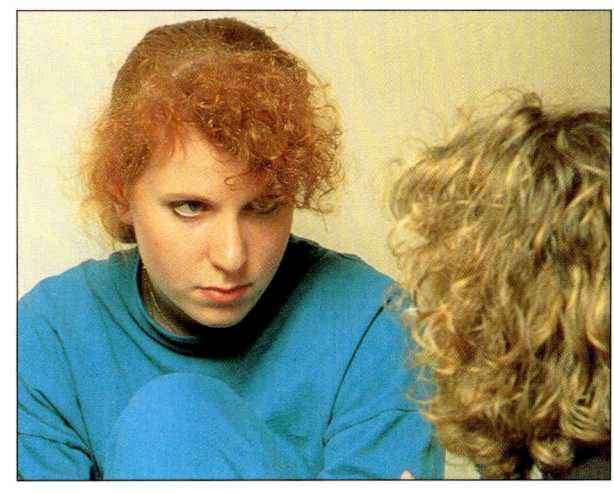

▲ Counselling can help people work out their problems so that they can drink less.

Some groups help people stop drinking completely. The most well known is called Alcoholics Anonymous. There are also groups which help families of alcoholics. (See the end of the book for details.)

Some people who have an alcohol problem can learn to drink normally again. For others, the only cure is to stop drinking and never drink again.

Like drug addiction, alcoholism is difficult to treat. But some alcoholics do get better and have a normal life again.

The laws on drinking

Like Annie, most children taste alcohol for the first time at home. But they cannot buy alcohol anywhere in Britain until they are sixteen. At sixteen they can buy beer or cider with a meal in a restaurant, but not wine or spirits. They cannot buy alcohol in a bar or shop until they are eighteen.

▼ On holiday, it's easy to forget the laws on drinking. Some countries are stricter than others.

Your parents can give you a drink at home at any time; it's only against the law to give alcohol to a child under five. If you are under fourteen, your parents can take you with them to a pub as long as there is a family room, away from the bar. Some pub owners allow teenagers into the bar between the ages of fourteen and eighteen but they cannot serve them a drink, even if an older person pays for it.

▲ These people are seventeen. They are too young to buy alcohol.

The rules are strict. Pub or restaurant owners who break the rules can lose their licence to sell alcohol which means they cannot work in a pub any more. The rules have to be strict because, as you have seen, drinking can make you ill and can be dangerous.

Of course drinking a lot makes adults ill too. But the governments that made the laws decided that people over eighteen are old enough to decide how much to drink. Some people never seem to learn. They make themselves ill again and again, and they upset the people around them by acting strangely. They also make themselves unhappy.

Prohibition

In 1919 the US government made it illegal to make, transport or sell alcohol. At that time there was a strong Temperance Movement in America. People who joined the Movement believed it was wrong to drink alcohol. They thought that people who drank alcohol were evil and likely to commit crimes, abuse their families and not respect God and the Church.

The Temperance Movement put pressure on the US government to ban alcohol. At the same time there were food shortages in some parts of the USA. The government decided that if it made it illegal to sell alcohol, this would please the Temperance Movement. At the same time, the grain used to make alcohol could be used for food instead.

▼ People who made alcohol when it was banned were called bootleggers.

The alcohol ban was called Prohibition. It did not work and it made crime worse. Hundreds of people made and sold alcohol illegally. Gangsters organized themselves into powerful groups to provide alcohol for hotels, restaurants and other places, where it was sold illegally. These groups fought each other to sell the most alcohol and make the most money. Some sold drugs and were involved in illegal gambling and prostitution too.

The police tried to enforce Prohibition. When they found places where alcohol was made, they destroyed them. But people quickly found other hiding places. The police also raided parties, clubs and restaurants where people were drinking and arrested anyone they could.

But the gangsters were too strong and too many ordinary people wanted to drink alcohol for the law to work. In 1933, the law was changed and people in the USA could buy and sell alcohol

▲ These Muslims only drink water with their meals. They are obeying Islamic laws.

again. Much of the crime which went with Prohibition disappeared.

Drinking alcohol is still illegal in some countries, usually for religious reasons. Under Islamic law Muslims are not supposed to drink alcohol and so it is banned in some countries of the Middle East. But many Muslims do drink alcohol, openly or in secret.

It is very difficult to stop people drinking alcohol if they really want to.

The risks people take

Janet is pregnant after having sex with the boy who took her home from the party. She is very sorry that she got drunk. But it's too late.

Women get drunk more quickly than men, even if they drink the same amount of alcohol. They also feel the effect for longer and they are more likely to damage their livers if they drink a lot. This is because they are smaller than men and have more fat and less water in their bodies, so alcohol affects them more.

When people get drunk they lose control. They do things that they would not normally do. When Janet got drunk she did something she would never have done if she hadn't been drinking. She accepted a lift alone in a car from a boy she hardly knew. She agreed to have sex with him and he did not wear a condom. She risked getting pregnant, and she could also have caught a sexual infection.

Even if she had said 'no' Janet might still have been in danger from this boy.

In fact, if she had gone home alone, Janet could still have been in danger. Being drunk, she could have fallen and hurt herself or, worse still, been knocked over by a car, and ended up in hospital.

Luckily, Janet wasn't attacked or hurt. But she is pregnant and she must make a difficult decision. Should she have the baby or have an abortion? If she decides to have the baby she will find it hard, at sixteen, to get 'A' levels. Going to university will be difficult, even with her family's help. Instead of going to parties and having fun with her friends she will have to stay home and look after her baby.

If she decides that she cannot cope with a baby when she is so young, Janet must face the hard decision to have an abortion.

▲ Janet doesn't know what to do. If only she hadn't drunk so much…

Alcohol and violence

One in four teenage boys get into arguments or fights after they have been drinking. One in ten get in trouble with the police. John's brother wasn't drunk but he was with people who were. What started as a friendly chat about football quickly turned into a nasty fight.

Alcohol can change people's moods very quickly. They can start an evening happy and laughing. But alcohol can make them depressed like Terry or angry and vicious like the people who hit John's brother.

▼ Things get out of control so quickly when you are drunk…

▲ …but it's too late for regrets now. The damage is done.

Before they know it, they lose control, like Janet, and do things they would never think of doing if they hadn't been drinking. Being drunk often leads to violence, vandalism, stealing or other crimes.

The boy who beat up John's brother was caught. His name was Keith and he was eighteen. Even though he had never been in trouble with the police before, he was sent to prison for three years. He was very sorry and could hardly believe what he had done. But the judge had to punish him because he had hurt John's brother so badly.

Keith will have a criminal record for the rest of his life. He will have trouble getting a job when he comes out of prison. Some countries, such as the USA, won't let him in because of his criminal record. Life will be very hard — all because he got drunk one night.

But John's brother is the victim. His eyesight is damaged. He had hoped to be a pilot when he left school. But his sight is too bad now. He must re-plan his future, just because Keith got drunk.

Drinking and driving

There have been laws about drinking and driving for over 100 years. People knew it was dangerous even to ride a horse after drinking a lot of alcohol.

In those days it was very difficult to measure the amount of alcohol in someone's blood. Now, police can use simple breath and blood tests.

During the early 1960s, studies in the USA showed that road accidents were more common when drivers had more than 80 mg of alcohol per 100 ml of blood in their bodies. The risk of accidents rose dramatically in those with over 100 mg alcohol per 100 ml of blood.

In 1967 a Road Safety Act was introduced in Britain which made it illegal to drive with a blood alcohol level above 80 mg per 100 ml. Many other countries

▶ A lot of people think that nobody should ever drink and drive.

have similar laws. In Britain, drivers caught with more than the legal blood alcohol level will lose their driving licence for at least twelve months. This means they cannot drive during that time. If they have been caught before, they will lose their licence for longer.

If a driver has a car accident when he or she has drunk too much and kills or even only slightly hurts someone, the driver may be sent to prison.

Even if no one is hurt, the driver could be put in a prison cell overnight, like Sharon's mum. It's a horrible thing to be locked up in a bare cell, with nothing to do but think about what has happened.

Anyone who drinks more than two pints of beer or half a bottle of wine is likely to have more than the legal level of alcohol in their blood. But some people will fail a breath test after drinking less and some won't fail it until they have drunk more.

It really is safest not to drink and drive at all.

Mixing alcohol and drugs

Drink and drugs don't mix well. Taking drugs such as cannabis, cocaine or heroin, is illegal with or without alcohol. Drugs can also be very dangerous. But taking medicines from the doctor or chemist with alcohol can be dangerous too. Alcohol can make drugs stronger and some drugs can add to the effects of alcohol.

If someone you know takes tranquillizing drugs, sleeping pills or anti-depressants, he or she should not drink alcohol. The alcohol will make the person sleepy and unable to concentrate. He or she might have, or cause, an accident.

Taking painkillers with alcohol can also be dangerous. Children under twelve should not take aspirin at all. But older people should not take it with alcohol as it can make their stomach bleed. Taking paracetamol with alcohol is a bad idea too; the mixture may damage the liver.

▲ Using equipment after drinking or with drugs is dangerous, as you can't concentrate properly.

Alcohol reacts badly with some drugs called antibiotics which are taken to fight infections. They can make you sick. Alcohol can also affect the drugs that people with diabetes take.

Some drugs do not work properly if you take them with alcohol. The alcohol makes your body break down the drugs too quickly, so they do not have a chance to work.

▼ Don't take medicines unless you know what they are for, and never mix them with alcohol.

It's best not to drink alcohol if the doctor has given you medicines to take, or you have bought some from the chemist. People who need to take medicines for a long time – for example, to treat asthma, high blood-pressure or arthritis – should ask their doctor if it is safe to drink.

Alcohol and the environment

Do you always put empty drinks cans and bottles in a bin? Or do you sometimes drop them on the ground?

▲ It's better to take rubbish home with you if there's nowhere to throw it.

If you throw cans on the ground they will stay there until someone picks them up. A dog or cat may cut itself on the sharp edge or swallow the ring pull and choke to death. If you drop a bottle, a child or an animal may cut itself on the broken glass. How would you feel if it was your little brother or sister or your dog or cat?

If all the empty cans that people in Britain throw away each year were placed end to end, they would reach the moon. That's nearly six billion cans. Cans are made from aluminium or tin plate. Both tin and aluminium are precious metals. Tin has to be mined and aluminium is made from bauxite in rocks. Both processes use a lot of energy. But recycling aluminium uses only 5 per cent of the energy it takes to make it, so it makes sense to recycle it, save energy and save the world's resources.

▲ This centre recycles old tins and cans, hundreds at a time.

In Sweden, 95 per cent of aluminium cans are recycled, and in the USA, over 50 per cent. In Britain we don't do nearly as well. We recycle less than 5 per cent of aluminium cans. The rest are thrown away. It's an awful waste.

Making glass also takes a lot of energy. We recycle more bottles than we used to but we are still a long way behind many countries.

Nowadays, most towns have bottle banks and some have special ways to collect tin and aluminium cans. You can find out about them by asking at the environment or refuse collection department at your Town Hall.

Everyone can help look after the environment.

Drinking sensibly

Most people like to drink alcohol sometimes, with their friends, with a meal or at a pub or party. There's nothing wrong with that. The important thing is to know when you've had enough so you can stop.

Some people only like one or two drinks, others want to drink much more. You've probably seen people who have had too much to drink. You've read that alcohol can make you ill, it can make you angry and violent, and it can cause accidents. So it makes a lot of sense not to drink too much.

An average British adult drinks about 240 pints of beer or lager in a year, 20 bottles of wine, 8 litres of cider and about 5 litres of spirits. It sounds an awful lot! You have to remember that this is over a whole year, and that as these are average figures, some people drink much less and some much more.

As some drinks contain more alcohol than others, alcohol is measured in units. Half a pint of beer is one unit and so is a small glass of wine or a single measure of gin, whisky or vodka.

No one knows exactly how much it is safe to drink. Doctors have said that women should not drink more than 14 units of alcohol per week and men should not drink more than 21. Pregnant women should drink as little as possible as alcohol can hurt the baby in the womb.

▼ You can have a good time with or without alcohol.

People can make sure they do not drink too much. If they are thirsty they can drink soft drinks before having any alcohol. If they mix wines and spirits with water or soft drinks, they will last longer and they will drink less alcohol.

Always sip alcoholic drinks, don't drink them down quickly like water, squash or cola. It's also a good idea to leave as much time as possible between each alcoholic drink.

Mixing different types of alcohol is a bad idea – it can make you drunk and sick very quickly. If you are offered punch or a drink you have not heard of, always check what's in it. If there are lots of things – gin, vodka, wine, brandy – keep well away!

But it's best to drink sensibly – or not at all – so alcohol is never a problem for you.

Glossary

Addiction When the body can't do without something.

Anti-depressants Drugs to treat people who are depressed.

Aspirin A painkilling drug that adults take for headaches and hangovers.

Ethanol The type of alcohol contained in drinks.

Fermentation The process by which microbes change starch into alcohol.

Germination The process by which a seed starts to grow roots, leaves, etc.

Illegal Against the law.

Liver The organ of the body which breaks down some of the body's waste products.

Microbe A tiny living organism which causes fermentation.

Paracetamol A drug used to treat headaches and hangovers.

Prostitution When a person sells their body for sexual purposes.

Tranquillizer A drug used to make people feel calmer.

Yeast A substance used to make beer and wine ferment, and bread rise.

Further information

Alcohol Concern
Waterbridge House
32–36 Loman Street
London SE1 0EE
Tel: 0171 928 7377
National charity that produces leaflets and information about safe drinking levels. It also has local groups that can advise on problem drinking.

Al-Anon Family Groups
61 Great Dover Street,
London SE1 4YF
Tel: 0171 403 0888
(24-hour confidential helpline)
For information and support to families of people with an alcohol problem.

Alateen
61 Great Dover Street
London SE1 4YF
Tel: 0171 403 0888
(24-hour confidential helpline)
For teenagers aged 12–20 whose lives are or have been affected by an alcoholic, usually a parent.

Drinkline
Tel: 0345 320202
(for the cost of a local call)
Dial and listen: 0500 801802
(FREEPHONE)
London only: 0171 332 0202
Information, advice and help, especially for young people.

Books to read

Alcohol by Pamela Holmes (Heinemann, 1991)

Alcohol by Iris Webb (Wayland, 1991)

Concerned about someone's drinking?
(available from Drinkline)

Substance Abuse by Y Solomon & J Coleman (Wayland, 1995)

What's Drunk, Mummy?
(available from Al-Anon Family Groups)

Index

accidents 5, 23, 24, 26, 28
alcoholism 13
antibiotics 24

beer 6, 14, 23, 28
blood 5, 8, 22-3
bootleggers 16
breath tests 22-3
brain 8, 10, 13
   cells 9, 10

cider 4, 10, 18, 21
counselling 13
crime 16-17, 21

depression 11, 20
driving 5, 22-3
drugs 13, 17, 24-5
drunkenness 4, 9, 10, 20

God 16
governments 15, 16

hangovers 10-11
heart 9

hospitals 5, 13

lager 28
laws 14-15, 17, 22-3
   Islamic 17
liver 9, 12-13, 18, 24

painkillers 11, 24
parties 4, 17, 18, 28
police 5, 17, 20-21, 22
prison 5, 21, 23
prostitution 17
pubs 5, 14-15, 28

recycling 26-7

sex 4, 18
spirits 14, 28-9

units of alcohol 28-9

violence 5, 17, 20-21, 28

wine 4, 6, 14, 23, 28-9